HUMAN FIGURES

✳

HUMAN FIGURES

❀

NANCY EIMERS

NEW MICHIGAN PRESS
TUCSON, ARIZONA

NEW MICHIGAN PRESS

DEPT OF ENGLISH, P. O. BOX 210067

UNIVERSITY OF ARIZONA

TUCSON, AZ 85721-0067

<http://newmichiganpress.com>

Orders and queries to <nmp@thediagram.com>.

ISBN 978-1-934832-87-5. FIRST PRINTING.

Design by Ander Monson.

Cover Photo 13377432 / Mannequin Hands ©
Dimitris Kolyris | Dreamstime.com

CONTENTS

Four Mannequins with Suitcases, Dressed for a Journey   1

Of Hands: Three 1960's Female Mannequins Dressed for Tea
    or Shopping, Posed with Artificial Birds   4

Photo of 50 Mannequins Posed in Front of the County Court
    House in Las Vegas, Nevada, Before the 1953 "Atomic Annie"
    Nuclear Test   6

Photo of Unnumbered Mannequins Piled in Front of the
    County Court House in Las Vegas, Nevada, After the 1953
    "Atomic Annie" Nuclear Test   8

One Side of a Leaf   10

After Reading Williams I Address the Doom Town Bomb Test
    Mannequins   12

ISIS Forces Iraq Shopkeepers to Veil Mannequins, or,
    Fragments Stolen from Shelley's "Mutability" and NBC
    News   14

Trees in a Parking Lot   15

On Gazing at Photos of Shopping Malls Dead and Living
    17

Bombed-out Mall in Baghdad, 2008   26

Fish take over the Bangkok New World Mall   27

Ghost Box, Label Scar   28

I Know Where Those People Went, They Went Down   30

On Being Human: A Consideration   31

Notes   35

Acknowledgments   37

FOUR MANNEQUINS WITH SUITCASES, DRESSED FOR A JOURNEY

I understand raindrops
    can distort the song of birds
so we may not know which direction
    the song is coming from,

but I don't understand the uncanny valley,
    the changeless faces of mannequins
or the factory owner who says
    she walks among their bodies

at night and is not afraid.
    Can they even be said
to have bodies? Made
    with care, she says, made individually

and I'm hearing affection not unlike
    how birds in cages begin to sing
when the shower comes on.
    Whatever they hear must resemble

something important by instinct;
    bodies, yes, in the sense of giving
form to what was once
    abstract. For instance, four mannequins

in travelwear, each figure's attitude
    an ode to patience, same as wasted
time, same timetable to read, same train
    about to come—the window sign *Vogue*

Suggests . . . then words too small
    to read without a telescope.
This might have mattered,
    what we wore on earth, faces they wore,

that bright *alert* urbanity
    makes out of poise—
and why we wanted them
    that way. The factory workers are sanding

haunches and torsos, tops of heads,
    anywhere a mannequin gets round
and the workers seem to do this respectfully,
    I swear. Of course they know

they are being filmed. A gentle roar
    is how I do not want
to describe the sound of falling water
    heard at a distance. Dull

instead of gentle doesn't get us
    any closer in a shopping mall
to why the mannequins all are headless now;
    headless has happened before,

it will happen again.
    We are passing through
yet another definition of apperception
    I do not quite understand,

instinct, a "prompting,"
    maybe why the heart recoils at what
resembles such composure—bright faces,
    pointless gestures—never to suppose

an end to come, not even lightly.

OF HANDS: THREE 1960'S FEMALE MANNEQUINS DRESSED FOR TEA OR SHOPPING, POSED WITH ARTIFICIAL BIRDS

Curves upon which one may hang
    a pocketbook, or which may be enclosed

inside a kidskin glove, if we include the wrist,
    express what Hogarth called

the waving line *as in flowers*, what
    I too shall call *the line of beauty*

though for what. Last week, on eBay: vintage female
    overall in great shape with some minor

wear when naked: faultline down the torso.
    Has both hands. Hand, though, first meant

human hand, later a means by which to measure
    the height of a horse. A hand that draws

a curving line would *take*
    a lively movement in making it.

So says Hogarth, silent then in the ever
    afterwards of hands with nothing to do,

half-open, poised, as if maybe
    the birds might fly back into them.

PHOTO OF 50 MANNEQUINS POSED IN FRONT OF THE COUNTY COURT HOUSE IN LAS VEGAS, NEVADA, BEFORE THE 1953 "ATOMIC ANNIE" NUCLEAR TEST

> *Fiberglass . . . currently the most widely used material for manufacturing mannequins . . . has a balanced ratio of weight and sturdiness.*

These objects, stable in form,
looking placid, maybe a little bit surprised

but calmly so, incurious
can be seen and touched

but can they be apprehended?
Behind the faces: facelessness,

this is where we go on storing anonymity.
Sitting—someone has seated them—

in folding chairs
all turned in the same direction

to look like an audience is waiting
for something that isn't happening.

These objects are not waiting
that in some other life

are ship hulls, longbows, drum sets,
Christmas tree angel hair.

PHOTO OF UNNUMBERED MANNEQUINS PILED IN FRONT OF THE COUNTY COURT HOUSE IN LAS VEGAS, NEVADA, AFTER THE 1953 "ATOMIC ANNIE" NUCLEAR TEST

Fiberglass. . . is not as resilient as a piece of solid wood,
but certainly stands up well to the relatively minimal
abuse that most department store mannequins experience.

those mannequins undamaged or not
                wiped off the face

are gathered / have been
                are dumped / set down

like burdens / *placed* here
                picnic-style if

picnickers were dying
                next to / over / under / across

each other not on blankets
                grayish stuff

a photograph has made
                of grass a heap of arms

still gesturing the
                fingers curled *please*

over come / sometime
    for morning / are you

welcome / tea was all
    distant politeness

could recall

ONE SIDE OF A LEAF

When I go to dredge something up on the computer today I must start with a photograph of Mladic in a baseball cap, looking up like a man surprised by the sound of someone speaking his name after hours of silence. He is being taken to the Hague to be put on trial. The story was posted thirty-five minutes ago. How will the present ever keep up with itself? The crime is old by some standards. It didn't happen overnight and involved many living souls; now it includes eight thousand deaths migrating home again like flocks of birds crossing the water from Whitefish Point to Canada. Later I will have to page backwards from some other present to get to this one.

*

Ten minutes later. The photograph is gone. Now it's *Egypt's Next Crisis*, a different photograph shows a man from the Muslim Brotherhood sitting in a coffee shop in front of a wall of photographs of men killed in Tahrir Square. Almost all of them smiling artlessly. Several are wearing glasses. It turns out "2011 Egyptian Revolution" is already an entry on Wikipedia, *the free encyclopedia that anyone can edit.* On Wikipedia's entry for "page or pages," the definition of *page* as *(paper)—one side of a leaf of paper, as in a book* appears near the bottom of the page (page?) after the categories Position or Occupation, Technology, Music, People, Fictional Characters, and Places, under Other Uses. To turn a page is to turn over an old leaf.

*

Politics, history. Ever getting away from us. *Saudi Arabia Struggles to Limit Region's Upheaval.* No, not *Struggles.* *Scrambles.* This means things are happening fast. In ten or twenty minutes another headline to be shrugged off to the bottom left or right of the page. I think of history as a schoolbook I am opening now so long ago. Politics used to be one kind of tickertape, now it's another. Like trying to hold a moonbeam in your hand.

*

What then is the present? Current is a flow of electrical charge carriers. My mother in Arizona used to be three hours behind. A woman I knew in Jordan is seven hours ahead. To an anonymous interviewer, I would like to say I am grieved to have missed our appointment but there was not a soul in the coffee shop, for it went out of business eons ago. I waited around in the parking lot: if quarter after five was the present, should I have waited a few minutes longer? Sometimes a parking lot is a broken watch.

AFTER READING WILLIAMS I ADDRESS
THE DOOM TOWN BOMB TEST MANNEQUINS

Begin, my friend, / for you cannot, / you may be sure,
take your song, / . . . / with you to the other world.

I wish I could befriend each one of you
        though even then and even if
    I asked you to begin

you could not say just how you came to be
        arranged so as to resemble a family
    of chairs in a waiting room.

I think there must be nothing much
        between you and some other world
    that may or may not come after this.

For instance, astronauts will train here
        after you are gone,
    a "crash course in geology,"

or, What We Might Expect to Find
        Upon the Moon. A surface maybe
    not unlike the blank

of your faces or the random cloudless
        pieces of sky in one of many
    jigsaw puzzles left unsolved

at the end of any
                profitless or merely cranky day,
          so that I really must have meant

begin as not having a chance in hell
                of finishing a single
          common

daily thing.

ISIS FORCES IRAQ SHOPKEEPERS TO VEIL MANNEQUINS, OR, FRAGMENTS STOLEN FROM SHELLEY'S "MUTABILITY" AND NBC NEWS

night closes round

the heads of she's
so elegantly wreathed

translucent black that ties in the back

the he's

how restlessly they speed

nowhere
in sporty poses

black CASCA bags yanked over their heads

as if their bodies hadn't heard
the breaking news

controlled a vast territory in the

human form

TREES IN A PARKING LOT

explore their anchorage
and pavement suffers,
broken lips or stub-toe spots.

*

This empty parking lot
this horselaugh—
doltish, inexpressive,
dazed, confounded—

tree-islands wonder-stuck—

*

Tree in a parking lot is for corporation.
Tree is for *throwing*
shade:
dissing a friend,
making a ghost.

*

Parking in back and on sides.
Parking in back.

No parking here.

Trees are for separation.
Trees, our dream

there were no cars,
there were no stores.
To want here is to be
surprised, then happy,

then alone.

ON GAZING AT PHOTOS OF SHOPPING MALLS DEAD AND LIVING

how harmless truth /is /in cold weather /to an empty nest
—A. R. Ammons

Italian Gold hung over
an empty shopwindow

—what can it mean?

BURT'S SHOES you can see clear through,
the letters gone,
pried out, maybe, by crowbar.

Black phone receiver hung
from a steel cord—

lost voice—the trail gone cold.

You have to find your store, a friend once said,
then buy all your clothing there.

In which of these deserted storefronts
should I dress myself—

Lancome, raids and Naturals, Underground Weather?

Ghost mall,
i.m. commerce:

In memoriam. Important Message.
Interested in meeting?

*

A nest acts like a pocket. It would fit inside one.
Basic meaning: sitting-place.

In this Hall of Waiting, men (almost always)
in cushy La-Z-Boys waited once, expecting
_____ to happen. Or: waited for a wife
or daughter to retrieve them. Or: waited. Not
expecting anything.

Starting with orange crates, men who invented the
La-Z-Boy called it "nature's way of relaxing." Seph
Lawless, photographer of abandoned places: "It
feels as though you're sitting outside yourself."

*

8 miles.
This is how far away we were

meant to be
from the radius of a nuclear blast.

8 miles out from Minneapolis
we'd shop without fear

that truth might come to us
out here at the introverted

Southdale Center ("pleasure dome
with parking": *Time*)

("a flight from Egypt":
Frank Lloyd Wright)

where even now there are others (strangers)
near enough, if not to touch.

                    *

Empty: containing little or nothing. Why so long
an entry in the dictionary? There are 14 definitions,
not to mention an empty bottle, an empty house,
empty streets, a life empty of happiness, an empty
head, the act of emptying water out of a bucket.
Not to mention means we are going to mention
it anyway so why pretend. The synonyms listed at
the end suggest additional categories: when empty
is itself the primary quality (a kind of purity);
when empty inspires a feeling of surprise; when
empty is temporary; when empty has to do with a
surface *free* of any markings (absence as a positive

state) or with the very fact of its having *yet to be* filled in (the pathos of expectation).

I put the book away. Empty—adding its little—

*

an ice cream parlor chair
in the ruins of a food court
on its side
the forsaken
moment someone
stood up asudden

*

Shoppers walking around in a brighter future didn't know it was also meant to serve as a fall-out shelter. "The most important factors are strength and support." Not to mention food and clothing, not to mention nature ("A Better Outdoors Indoors"), fifty-foot eucalyptus trees in the center court, exotic birds in cages, a petting zoo. Steel and reinforced concrete would offer protection from matter vaporized by a fireball, condensed in the rain and turned to radioactive dust. Tents could be pitched in the parking lot.

*

13, 14, 15 feet,
the giant gator of Buffalo Creek Golf Course

has roamed the links for years,
and he's apparently good for business.

Walking allowed: yes
Pro shop available: yes.

We never saw the monster Alligator
but had a great day and great time out on the course.

Visa, MasterCard: yes.
Tank tops, mid shirts, cutoffs: no.

The pro shop staff was excellent
and accommodated all of our needs.

*

At Twelve Oaks Mall, we installed eight 24' replica Pin
Oak trees in the Grand Court. We were able to custom
build these trees with unique branches with foliage that
were accented with shades of green and yellow to add
additional realism to the trees. The theme of naturalism
is carried throughout the shopping mall . . . .

*

Ruptured ceilings, bluish sheen of glass
beneath a broken skylight—

light that gets in anyhow
just makes me bluer than hell,

the living vines
still crawling sideways out of a twentieth century

atrium.
The escalator at Coney Island

was ridden by 75,000 pleasure-seekers,
this one brought back

down to earth by a heavy snow.

*

Southlake Mall has a 60-foot river running through
it—you can walk on water—a series of digital panels
laid horizontally, beside them the vertical digital
panels of trees, *bringing technology and nature together
for shoppers*. You can skip a virtual stone over virtual
waters, or "catch" a virtual salmon: capture or seize;
reach just in time, so as to carry away.

Shop in 1300
meant a booth or shed for work

by way of scyppen—
cowshed.

1764—to shop (with intention to buy)
took centuries.

By 1924 one
shopped around.

In 1956 someone first mentions
a shopping cart. Mom,

I can still imagine us driving around
down there in the black and white photograph of a parking lot

taken by chopper
hovering over Woodfield Mall—

you and me inside a matchbook car
as indistinguishable from the others

as snowflakes.

*

It is said that Piranesi dreamed up his *Imaginary Prisons* while delirious with a fever, catwalks, bridges, statues, ominous ropes and hanging chains, the monumental Romanesque interiors. Space is the jailer. Fear of open spaces. Time is the stairways lofting upwards, ending nowhere. Fear of looking up. Light appears as blocks of marble trapped by crosshatching. Fear of being touched. If you are interested enough to enlarge a portion of any one of the etchings, go ahead—you may begin to feel the madness, ladders / balustrades / the tiny figures (jailers? prisoners?) / capstans / archways looming into angry scribbles. You have to back off then: I need you at enough of a distance to see how much this looks like the Galleria in Houston, Texas. Do we wake or sleep?

*

This is all it was

ever going to be

—more—

space, capacity for . . .

even our desertion

falling

short.

BOMBED-OUT MALL IN BAGHDAD, 2008

Maybe we weren't looking far enough into the future.
    There. Just over the ruler-line of horizon.

Cross between a deserted parking garage and a colosseum,
    a mesh of rebar holding the nothing in tension.

In the *right exactly now* of photojournalism
    soldiers are climbing an escalator forever

stopped in its tracks, two more on the rooftop, each taking a knee
    to survey the city, if neither guy can be wholly sure

what the other is seeing. It's a peaceful disagreement between them.
    And below, that filtered light, how it chances

on some things rather than others. Broken stair.
    Brick column, gravel, combat boot. Windows of light

float over the basement water's sickly green. Bent leg of a soldier
    stepping down. That mottled camo is meant to break up

outlines, disappear an ankle, wrist or knee. Maybe
    the ghosts of future shoppers looking back

will see us as commonplace, merely a hole in the chatter.

FISH TAKE OVER THE BANGKOK NEW WORLD MALL

after the fire
set by a business competitor or (building code violations)
            official ghost

devoured the roof
so light gets in through stories and stories
            down to the koi and carp, catfish, tilapia and mango fish

swimming around and around
in the basement rainwater, skirting escalators and concrete
    stanchions,
            a species of glimmer seems to be

taking over the murk//
you'll have to sneak around the police
            just to enter that dreamy feeling

someone called ruin porn
and be all the more
            apart for their furtiveness

is and is not ours//

27

GHOST BOX, LABEL SCAR

It is not at peace, but what is peace?
Dead leaves, maybe a river—

grass in the cracks of a parking lot.
That was never a reason,

never a lonely reason.
Fountains, bridges, skylights,

was it something about taking off?
Some peace is more formal than others.

Some is just about being here.
Mannequins, most of them are composed

of plastic or fiberglass.
They don't quite look at you.

Really, they are made out of distance.
I wouldn't want to walk in there at night.

I wouldn't even want to call it
night. Tree growing out of a window.

How did it get inside in the first place?
Or was it a seed blown in, like a horse

lowered into a mine as a foal?
Ghost box, label scar—

If there are ghosts, they can't remember
why they are naked, how they got that way.

I KNOW WHERE THOSE PEOPLE WENT, THEY WENT DOWN

Again tonight the players follow the Old French *arc*
of a baseball under the stadium lights that go on
trying to answer our many needs in a different way
than lights that shine on billboards and freeway signs
or over parking lots. The empty seats are talking
of money, the money is talking emptily from hand
to hand. On a night like this the moon has nothing
to do but remember itself to the car hoods
and fenders and the little else a parking lot can
shine back up. I would wish someone to have
one of those expensive empty seats. The red seams press
on the hand as the pitch is preparing itself to fly.
Late summer nights I open my window
and hear the bleary roar of trucks on I-94
and think how there may be sleepers out there
burrowed in sleeping bags beneath an overpass
and maybe over their heads are the mud nests
built a mouthful of mud at a time.
Cliff swallows once were murdered by cars
but are flying these days with a shorter wingspan,
that they may turn and pivot and roll away with a swiftness
trouble had to teach them over the generations.

ON BEING HUMAN: A CONSIDERATION

Someone is walking awhile
    in the freshness that is supposed
to be morning
            inside yet another millennial shopping mall
where under fluorescence the expectations
    of say a row of light blue Oxford shirts on their hangers
can be breathtaking
                almost—

I know. I have wanted
    to fling myself into their arms
almost exhausted. Almost home.

Almost fifty-seven, my face
    is beginning to look
like its father. I feel the eyes tightening
            and the pouches yearn.
Here, look, there are couches, and chairs
    inviting anyone
to recline. There are people passing
            who look like they never
                light.

I am nearing my birthday.
                        Let me walk ahead

a little ways. Get my bearings,
     wade hip-deep into what was once
a marsh with trees.
          Shoes and earrings, careworn faces,
                    isn't it all
a common dreaminess? If so, will you wait?

I'd like to stop by those trees.

NOTES

The epigraph on fiberglass in "Photo of 50 Mannequins Posed in Front of the County Court House in Las Vegas, Nevada, Before the 1953 'Atomic Annie' Nuclear Test" quotes Bianca Bumpres.

The epigraph in "Photo of Unnumbered Mannequins Piled in Front of the County Court House in Las Vegas, Nevada, After the 1953 'Atomic Annie' Nuclear Test" is taken from a posting on mannequinstore.com.

"On Gazing at Photos of Shopping Malls Dead and Living": the block of italicized prose appears in "The Power of a 'Green' Mall," http://www.ambius.com/blog/the-power-of-a-green-mall. "A Better Outdoors Indoors" is the title of an essay in *Architectural Record* (June, 1962) on America's first indoor shopping center. "The most important factors are strength and support": "Building Your Bombshelter," http://undergroundbombshelter.com. The comment about the giant alligator that is "apparently good for business" is taken from Ashley Forest and Marvin Clemon's article, "Giant Gator Roams Golf Course in Florida," May 26, 2016, KSNV News Las Vegas. The two italicized responses to the Buffalo Creek Golf Course were posted on Golf Advisor.com. The source of "bringing technology and nature together for shoppers" is https://www.shoppingsouthlakemall.com/thedocks, an ad for said mall.

"Ghost box" is a term for an empty retail store. "Labelscar": when the lettering from the store sign is removed and there is a readable residue or fading left behind in the dust and dirt.

"I Know Where Those People Went, They Went Down"—the title of this poem is an excerpt from something James Wright said during a 1968 poetry reading in Montreal.

ACKNOWLEDGMENTS

Grateful acknowledgment is made to the following magazines in which some of these poems appeared, sometimes with different versions/titles:

Alaska Quarterly: "Ghost Box, Label Scar," "Four Mannequins with Suitcases, Dressed for a Journey"

Connotation Press: An Online Artifact: "One Side of a Leaf"

Crazyhorse: "Bombed-out Mall in Baghdad," "ISIS Forces Iraq Shopkeepers to Veil Mannequins, or Fragments Stolen from Shelley's 'Mutability' and NBC News"

Dunes Review: "Being Human: A Consideration"

FIELD: "Photo of 50 Mannequins Posed in Front of the County Court House in Las Vegas, Nevada, Before the 1953 'Atomic Annie' Nuclear Test," "Photo of Unnumbered Mannequins Piled in Front of the County Court House in Las Vegas, Nevada, After the 1953 'Atomic Annie' Nuclear Test"

Gettysburg Review: "Of Hands: Three 1960's Female Mannequins Dressed for Tea or Shopping, Posed with Artificial Birds," "After Reading Williams I Address the Doom Town Bomb Test Mannequins"

Seattle Review: "On Gazing at Photos of Shopping Malls, Dead and Living"

To Bill, abiding love and thanks.

NANCY EIMERS is the author of four previous poetry collections, *Oz*, *A Grammar to Waking*, *No Moon*, and *Destroying Angel*. Her poems have appeared in numerous magazines and anthologies, and she has been the recipient of a *Nation* "Discovery" Award, a Whiting Writers Award, and two NEA Fellowships. She lives in Kalamazoo, Michigan.

❀

COLOPHON

Text is set in a digital version of Jenson, designed by Robert Slimbach in 1996, and based on the work of punchcutter, printer, and publisher Nicolas Jenson. The titles here are in Futura.

✻

NEW MICHIGAN PRESS, based in Tucson, Arizona, prints poetry and prose chapbooks, especially work that transcends traditional genre. Together with DIAGRAM, NMP sponsors a yearly chapbook competition.

DIAGRAM, a journal of text, art, and schematic, is published bimonthly at THEDIAGRAM.COM. Periodic print anthologies are available from the New Michigan Press at NEWMICHIGANPRESS.COM.

CPSIA information can be obtained
at www.ICGtesting.com
Printed in the USA
LVHW110732310322
714755LV00001B/121